© Copyright by CASA EDITRICE PLURIGRAF
S.S. Flaminia, km 90 - 05035 NARNI - TERNI - ITALIA
Tel. 0744 / 715946 - Fax 0744 / 722540 - (Italy country code: +39)
All rights reserved. No Part of this publication may be reproduced.
Printed: 1996 - PLURIGRAF S.p.A. - NARNI

Petra has been described in a thousand different ways by its numerous visitors. Each portrayal has encountered the same difficulty in transforming into words the very special sensations aroused by this unique city.

It has been said that Petra is as red as a rose and as old as time, or that it is a city that has been kept alive to honour its dead, or that the different colours of the rocks give the impression of travelling through a rainbow. Perhaps no one will ever be able to explain the way in which the visitor is rendered speechless with admiration in seeing all those rock sculptures almost as they were when first carved, being such testimonies to human skill.

In 1812 Burckhardt, a Swiss explorer, became the first European to give account of Petra. His first impression was that of an immense priceless treasure jealously preserved in its rocky coffer. He had heard people speaking of a mysterious city hidden among impenetrable mountains and during one of his several expeditions in the Arabian desert, in order to justify his search for that forgotten city, he disguised himself as a Muslim (he knew perfect Arabic) wishing to make a sacrifice on the tomb of the prophet Aaron, which he knew was in that area. As soon as the narrow Siq gorge opened to reveal its secret, Burckhardt had no further doubts: it was the legendary Petra, capital of the Nabataeans, an Arab population that ruled over the Transjordan area before the Roman conquest.

There is very little information concerning the Nabataeans: we only know that they were nomads and that they settled in this region of present day Jordan at the end of the 7th century B.C. prospering with the trade of spices. It has also been suggested that they were a form of desert highwaymen who made their living plundering the passing caravans. In any case, this population was able to

extend its territory and to settle there permanently ·because of some of the region's favourable features such as an abundance of water and its natural position, strategically protected from the enemies by its high and inaccessible mountains.

The Nabataeans, who were mainly nomads, took a long time to get used to a definitive settlement, but Petra had an enormous advantage: its position.

Petra was at the junction of the main caravan routes for spices, silk and frankincense coming from China, India and Arabia, and then continuing towards Egypt and the Mediterranean, and it represented an ideal place to stop and trade.

The abundance of water, cunningly kept in thousands of water tanks that can be found almost everywhere in

the city and in its neighbourhood, was the prime reason for the passing caravans to stop there.

Consequently, the city became a trading centre for all the goods that converged there and, as a result, the Nabataeans suffered little in their transition from a nomadic to a settled lifestyle. Furthermore, they benefitted directly from the trade by imposing taxes on all the goods that passed through Petra in exchange for the hospitality and protection of the city.

They quickly learned that successful trade depended upon having a stable and secure environment, the-, refore they always kept on friendly terms with the neighbouring peoples.

Subsequently, their settling in Petra enabled them to worship their gods, Dushara and his wife Al'Uzza, erecting for them wonderful temples. Their gods were closely connected with water, which was the chief fertility symbol for the Nabataeans, and many animals were offered as sacrifice to them. Evidence of this can be seen in the several stone altars used for sacrifice, where the shedding of blood, as the vital liquid and symbol of the regeneration of man, represented the desire to renew continuously the relationship between god and man.

The major splendour of the Nabataean kingdom was from the 1st century B.C. to the 1st century A.D., when the city reached its highest population of almost 3.000 inhabitants. It was at that time that the Romans, who were attracted by its power and wealth, decided to annex that area and the kingdom became part of the Roman province of Arabia.

A new development of the city derived from the union between the Nabataean and Roman cultures: the theatre was enlarged, the buildings

were enriched with decorations that admirably merged the different architectural styles, and the main road was paved and adorned with a triumphal arch.

However, this flourishing period did not last for long because as the Roman control increased in the region, the commercial routes became redirected and rarely passed through Petra. As a consequence the Nabataeans gradually lost their influence.

The second empire that settled in Petra was that of the Byzantines during the 6th century A.D., which introduced Christianity. Petra became a diocese and many buildings were turned into churches.

Later, Petra was plagued by a long series of earthquakes which caused people to think that it was no longer the safe city of its prosperous past, and its most recent traces of stable residences in the city are some fortifications that the Crusaders erected on Al-Habis hill in the 12th century A.D..

Consequently, Petra became just a stopping place for caravans and, in the following centuries, only the local Bedouins lived there.

Nowadays, only small dealers selling to tourists live in Petra.

Finally, we should not forget how much this place is associated with references and happenings that are legendary and famous from the stories of the Bible: it is here that Moses made water gush from the rock which he struck in order to quench his people's thirst during the hard journey towards the Promised Land. Today we still find the Altar where Abraham intended to sacrifice his son Isaac in honour of God. In addition, tradition has it that the prophet Aaron was buried here.

Do we need any further excuses to plunge into the atmosphere of Petra? Surely not. It is time to begin our journey.

The Siq gorge

There have been few changes since those days when the ancient caravans entered Petra: nowadays, just as before, in order to cross the threshold of the city one has to weave through the Siq gorge, a narrow and winding chasm the origins of which are uncertain as to whether having been caused by the *Wadi Mousa* torrent or a geological fracture.

One experiences an unmistakable feeling of mystery when walking or riding through the passage: the height of its limestone faces which change from rosy to grey according to the time of the day, its sudden narrowing, the constant passing of the Bedouins, often at full gallop and wrapped in a cloud of dust: all contribute to create the highly captivating atmosphere of the site.

At one time, a monumental **Triumphal Arch**, erected in honour of the Roman emperor Adrianus visiting the Arab province, dominated the entrance into the valley, whereas now only some vertical ruins are visible.

Entering the gorge one notices a series of niches and tabernacles probably dedicated to Atargatis, goddess of fertility and life. Further on attention is then caught by a group of cubes carved out of rock, called **Djin Blocks**. The word *djin* in Arabic means "spirit" and it is thought that they were cut from the rock as a dwelling place for the Nabataean spirit-guardians. This type of construction was considered a divine fertility gift and can always be found in close proximity to water courses.

The most interesting monument lying on the Eastern side of the Siq is the **Obelisk Tomb**, so called because of the presence of four obelisks that rise above the tomb's entrance and constitute a typical element of Nabataean funeral monuments. They represented symbols of divine presence for this people

The Siq – *Impressive entrance way to the city of Petra*

Another view of the Siq gorge, with its limestone rocks that change colour from rosy to grey when lit by the sun.

and, since there are four and not one, as is generally the case, we can infer that they were carved out of the rock to honour four gods.

Below the tomb there is the **Triclinium**, adorned with columns, lintels and pediments. Many of the tombs that can be admired in Petra have this hall in which were held banquets in honour of the dead.

The route along the Siq is long and not particularly easy whether by horse or on foot. Nowadays, there are almost no remains of the once magnificent limestone cubes that paved it, however this does not distract from the beauty of the remaining features, such as when the corridor opens and the sun pierces inside to light the rose-red rocks. In spring, in addition to visual sensations there is the intense fragrance of the white broom and the pungent smell of aloe, while bushes of pink oleanders elegantly adorn the sides of the path.

Two examples of the lush vegetation that adorns the Siq pathway in spring.

A group of Djin Blocks, cube shaped rocks which, according to Nabataean tradition, were the dwelling-place of the city's spirit-guardians.

The Obelisk Tomb.
The four obelisks that rise above it symbolize some Nabataean deities. Below the tomb there is the Triclinium.

The Siq seen from Al - Khazneh Farun.

The strongest emotion comes just when the visitor wonders whether the Siq gorge will ever come to an end. As if by magic, the ravine discloses to the traveller what is perhaps the most spectacular of the monuments preserved in Petra: **Al-Khazneh Farun** (Treasure of the Pharaoh). It is completely carved in the rock and it is believed to have been the tomb of King Harith IV (84-85 B.C.). It is almost perfectly preserved by being secluded in a place particularly protected from the atmospheric elements.

Its elegant and refined lines make it one of the best rock sculptures of this site. The façade is divided in two storeys and the features that decorate it represent the typically Nabataean style harmoniously blending with others in classical style, such as the statues, the Corinthian capitals and the pediment that surmounts the columns. At the top, in the middle, there is the *thòlos*, a small circular temple with a dome-shaped roof, adorned with three statues.

In comparison to the majestic entrance the interior is rather disappointing because it consists of a single square and bare chamber flanked by two smaller rooms and by another one at the rear.

Its name derives from a legend stating that some thieves once hid their treasure in the urn located in the centre of the second floor. As a matter of fact, many people must have believed in this legend if one judges from the several bullet marks visible on the urn that decorates the top of the tomb, obviously fired in the attempt to capture that legendary treasure.

The best time to appreciate the red colouring of its carved rock is around 10 am.

Al-Khazneh Farun *is one of Petra's best preserved monuments.*

Left – The striking façade of Al - Khazneh Farun **seen from the Siq.**

Below – The typical Nabataean features of the central urn in Al - Khazneh Farun (Treasure of the Pharaoh) **made many people believe that a treasure was hidden in it.**

The Theatre

Not far from Al-Khazneh the visitor finds the **Theatre**, built by the Nabataeans at the beginning of the 1st century A.D.. It was subsequently enlarged by the Romans when the kingdom was annexed in 106 A.D.. It represents the only example of a theatre excavated from rock among all the Roman theatres recovered in the ruled territories.

It has been recently discovered that the pink sandstone was cut to create seats for up to 8000 spectators in 33 concentric semicircles.

In order to make more space and afterwards to improve the acoustics of the site the Romans destroyed many adjacent houses and tombs, and the squared hollows that we can see above are what remains of the burial niches that were desecrated for their passion for drama.

*The **unusual** Roman Theatre, **the only one of its kind directly carved out of rock.***

"Blood, arena and Pantomimes in Petra"

What sort of performances might a theatre with more than 7000 seats have staged in Petra?

Certainly, some shows must have been of a cultural nature, such as readings of poetry or displays by rhetoricians visiting Petra. However, the main reason why the inhabitants of Petra would go and sit for several hours on the uncomfortable seats of that theatre was to see something really thrilling or enjoyable and well worth the entry price: for example, a good fight between gladiators and wild ferocious beasts with its associated abundant spilling of blood, or a good *pantomime* with songs and dances, when feeling in a more charitable mood.

A *pantomimus* was a single actor that was able to imitate all things, to dance, to sing and to hold the audience's attention, supported only by musicians and chorus. He was not a particularly sophisticated artist and in order to be successful it was necessary for him to have a large quantity of well tested witty remarks and tricks ready to amuse and amaze the audience. Even if they were not highly considered by the authorities, who regarded that profession disreputable, the most skilled actors were often very rich and famous.

On the other hand, it was more difficult for gladiators to become famous because their high mortality rate did not allow them to perform for more than two or three times, when lucky. If they were professional gladiators, trained in special schools, their skills might allow them to survive more fights.

The **High Place of Sacrifice** rests on the top of the *Attouf Ridge* and is "conquered" after a strenuous walk up paths and staircases, which were once part of the sacred Nabataean road.

The platform is distinctly divided in two parts: in the first one facing South we see two high **obelisks** of rock piercing the sky and dominating the terrace. They were modelled by levelling the surrounding rock, and, according to some scholars, they symbolize the two most important Nabataean deities *Dushara* and Al'U*zza*.

The part facing North contains the ruins of a **fort** that was built in order to control the approaches to the area, and **Abraham's Altar** which, according to the local legend, was to be used for the sacrifice of his son, Isaac.

This place of sacrifice is quite small, suggesting that it was never intended as an area that could contain large crowds. It is probably the best preserved sacrificial site.

The *altar* itself, where the priest cut the throats of the sacrificial beasts, is about the size of an average church altar and is approached by three steps.

On the upper surface of the altar the visitor can see a square hollow

*The High Place of Sacrifice, **on the top of the Attouf Ridge.
In the centre there is the Mensa Sacra used for bloodless offerings.***

which held a black stone, probably a meteorite, symbolizing Dushara and which channelled his power through the victims blood during the ritual ceremonies as it flowed away through specially cut channels.

The rock around the altar was carved to create a small courtyard surrounded by tiers of seats, as in a *triclinium*.

In front of the altar there is a very low platform, only a few centimeters high, the **Mensa Sacra**, for bloodless offerings.

This is one of the obelisks **on the top of the Attouf Ridge. It was modelled by levelling the surrounding rock. For the Nabataeans the obelisk typically symbolized a deity; in this case it could represent Dushara or Al'Uzza.**

"Nabataean Deities"

The Nabataeans were a population of Arab origin, of nomadic characteristics and belonging to the Aramaean culture. This can be deduced from the inscriptions that were found in some tombs and temples and that were written in a language certainly deriving from Aramaean.

Their religion, too, emphasizes Aramaean elements, together with Arab reminiscences of the pre-Islamic period, bringing the scholars to define it a "synthesized" religion.

Both the Greeks and the Romans believed that the Nabataeans had a type of cult derived from the union of very different elements, because of the continual contact between this people and other civilizations located between the Persian Gulf and the Mediterranean Sea. From these other cultures the Nabataeans borrowed the deities that in some way were associated with fertility and abundance.

The reason is evident: an arid land like that on which Petra was founded was difficult to cultivate and to make fertile, therefore it was considered essential to win the favour of the prosperity gods and offer them sacrifices in return for abundant harvests and water.

The main Nabataean god was **Dushara**, lord of life, who was compared to the Sun itself according to solar worship which was widespread throughout the Middle-East. In Greece we find him under the name of **Dusare**, but the name varies from time to time, as Herodotus testifies when discussing the Arab cults of Petra's area. In the meantime he identifies him with Dionisus, but also finds additional references to the god under the names of *Orotat, Dusares, Dushrat, Dusara-Ara*. The latter name means "Lord of Shara" and very probably refers to the mountains of el - Shara that are situated North of Petra.

According to the news that reached us, he was a benevolent male deity, of propitiating virtues, responsible for the welfare of the people that worshipped him. For the Nabataeans he represented the moment of maximum vigour in the reproductive cycle of nature: that when fruit is picked. His symbol was a black stone (*betyle*) placed on a squared rock, on which sacrificial blood was probably poured; this type of sacred stone was always found were sacrifices were being held.

The Nabataean feminine deity, initially simply called **Allat** ("the goddess"), subsequently took on various names and in Petra she adopted that of **Al' Uzza** (the "powerful"). Her symbol was the Moon or the planet Venus, the evening star; the animals dedicated to her were the lioness, the cow and sometimes the snake.

She symbolized receptivity and ruled over the course of human life and the alternation of the seasons; everything depended on her will: the outcome of a battle, the subsiding of storms, the awakening of nature in spring. Furthermore, she was the goddess of water and fertility.

Among the other deities of Nabataean cult there are **Atargatis**, harvest and abundance goddess, with whom Al'Uzza is often associated, and **Manat**, Allat's sister, that presided over fate and fortune.

After having admired the superb view from the high ground of the Attouf Ridge, during the descent towards the city you can observe the **Lion Fountain**, the sacred beast of Al'Uzza, on the pathway in the Farasa valley. This impressive monument was originally a fountain and was intended to refresh the pilgrims heading towards the place of sacrifice.

Unfortunately, the lion's head has been severely weathered by the continuous flow of water from the mountain above.

In this zone there are some very interesting tombs and buildings.

The **Garden Temple** is characterised by a terrace carved out of the rock consisting of two half-columns and two columns which are still in perfect condition and still well able to support the weight overhead. It

can be considered a rarity in Petra to find something like this still in its original position. The hypogeum, with a vaulted roof, contains about twelve niches carved in the walls.

The **Tomb of the Roman Soldier** is on the level below and the open space in front of it is the *Triclinium*, which was once joined to the tomb by a colonnaded courtyard. The façade is adorned with four columns, and the noticeably protruding pedi-

The Garden Temple.

Above – *The Tomb of the Roman Soldier.*

Right – *The Tomb of the Roman Soldier:* **this is the inside of the Triclinium** *carved from the multi-coloured rock that is characteristic of all the tombs in Petra.*

The Renaissance
Tomb.

ment has an unusually almost flattened top.

Its name derives from the three statues positioned in the niches between the columns, portraying some Roman legionaries, and it could have been erected for an important personage towards the 2nd century A.D., after the city's annexation to the empire.

The *Triclinium* is the only one of its kind in Petra with a carved interior decoration: its big hall is adorned with alternating niches and semicolumns that seem to emerge mightily from the rock, while pink, red and blue striations spread across all the walls creating a unique effect.

The **Renaissance Tomb** is probably the most architecturally sophisticated tomb. It is upwardly projected and has an elaborate vault adorned with pinnacles. This is in contrast with the outer decorations which are soberly finished with simple capitals.

The **Broken Pediment Tomb** was apparently damaged by an earthquake. It was carved from a lateral outcrop of rock which is centrally indented. It can be reached from a staircase of twelve steps.

The Broken Pediment Tomb.

Left – The Façade Street - *a section in detail.*

Below – The Façade Street *as seen in the distance from the Colonnaded Street. There, a series of some of the most interesting tombs in Petra are situated one next to the other; their magnificence and elegance remain intact, despite the effects of passing time.*

The heart of the city is the **Colonnaded Street** that represented the *cardo maximus* of the city at the time of Roman presence. The cardo - in North/South direction - constituted together with the decumanus - in East/West direction - the basis of the road structure that outlined the Roman urban settlements.

Along this street you come to the ruins of the semicircular **Nymphaeum**, which is located exactly where the *Wadi al Mataha* and the Wadi Mousa rivers join. It served as a public fountain and was devoted to the water nymphs.

All that remains of the old paved street are dazzling white limestone blocks that finish where the Greek-Roman ruins of the majestic **Temenos Gate** were recovered. The visitor can notice some extremely well preserved decorative features, such as low-reliefs, sculptures, geometrical and animal-shaped designs of Nabataean taste, and bordering tower-columns. It is surely an interesting example of how two different cultures, the Roman and the Nabataean complemented each other. Recent studies consider it to be the entrance gate to the Qsar al - Bint Temple.

On the left of the street, heading towards the Temple, three ancient market sites of Petra were identified, the upper, middle and lower markets, better known by their collective name of **Trajan's Market**.

Between the area used for the market and the big entrance gate to Qsar al - Bint the so-called **Great Temple of Dushara** was recently discovered. We can only infer that it must have been an impressive com-

The Colonnaded Street, situated in the centre of the lower part of the city. It ran North to South, dividing the city in half.

The Temenos Gate.
The remains of this majestic entrance, which probably led to Qsar Al - Bint Temple, reveal the delicate flower- and animal-shaped Nabataean designs that ornate the Roman style columns, emphasizing how the Roman and the Nabataean cultures successfully merged together in Petra for a long period.

plex, judging by the size of the columns recovered in the excavations. Some scholars also suggests that the structure could even have been the city *Forum* or *Agorà*.

On the right side of the street are the remains of the **Byzantine Tower**, the **Royal Palace** and the **Temple of the Winged Lions**.

The latter, which is at the moment being excavated, was presumably erected around 27 B.C. and gets its name from the carved lions placed on the column capitals. It is, however, devoted to the goddess Al'Uzza, also known as Atargatis, who was Dushara's wife and fertility goddess.

Right – *Another glimpse of the* Colonnaded Street. **In the foreground there are the remains of the paved street with dazzling white limestone blocks that once led to the Temenos Gate.**

Below – *The Temenos* Gate: *the flower-shaped decorations in detail.*

The Temenos Gate: its ruins.

Temple of the Winged Lions. **The temple, which is presently being excavated, was dedicated to the fertility goddess Atargatis, notwithstanding its name.**

Qsar Al Bint Temple

Qsar Al - Bint Temple (Castle of the Pharaoh's Daughter) is the only remaining example in Petra of a building which has not been carved from the rock.

It was built in the period between 30 and 40 B.C. and it measured 23 meters in height. Up until the discovery of the other temple, it was considered to have been the main Nabataean place of worship in the city. However, now the doubt has arisen as to whether it was a temple, a fortress or the dwelling of a princess. Presently, most people adhere to the theory that it was a temple, even if the local Bedouins romantically describe a tale of an Egyptian princess (hence the name) that once lived there and who had promised to marry the man who would succeed in supplying her palace with water.

It is important to take notice of H*arith* IV's inscription on the South wall of the sacred courtyard (*Temenos*) informing us that the building was once owned by the king.

The façade was presumably adorned with a pediment decorated with geometrical reliefs resting on six square-sided columns. The interior of the building consists of three parts, of which the central chamber was considered to be sacred and presumably contained the statue of the god, which for the Nabataeans was represented by a rectangular block of rock, the *betyle*, with stylized eyes, nose and mouth engraved on it. Only later, under the Greek-Roman influence, did the Nabataeans abandon this custom and from the 2nd century A.D. they took to representing their deities in the shape of statues.

The two lateral rooms were most probably used for carrying out indoor religious cerimonies, whereas the staircases inserted in the lateral walls led to the open-air terraces where the tradition of sun rituals, devoted to the deities of the cult of the Sun, required that those ceremonies be held.

Ruins of the Qsar al - Bint. **In Petra it is considered an unusual construction because it was built and not cut from rock.**

The Royal Tombs

In the Eastern side of the city there are some of the most spectacular monuments in Petra, the so-called **Royal Tombs**. They are carved into the face of the *Jabal·Khubtha* mountain, what is considered the Wall of the kings, but nobody really knows who these kings were, or whether these monuments, fashioned in such a masterly way, were tombs, temples or simply rich dwellings. In any case they are universally known as tombs, the first of which is the **Urn Tomb**, one of the grandest and most sophisticated among those present in Petra.

It was presumably cut out of the rock around 70 A.D., and is surrounded on the sides by a deep colonnade, unfortunately badly weathered, that overlooks a wide courtyard. This original design was evidently too small because the courtyard had been subsequently enlarged by extending it onto a platform, boldly resting on an elaborate system of arches, as was discovered in 1936 by the archaeologist Albright.

The legend has it that each arch would contain a cell where prisoners would be confined.

The façade is a good example of classical Nabataean decorative simplicity, in which the clear and perfect lines are still in almost perfect original condition.

The inner hall (hypogeum) is exceptionally majestic. It contains th-

The Urn Tomb.

The Urn Tomb - the
façade in detail.

The Palace Tomb

ree niches towards the rear and some alcoves along the sides. The entrance is through the door in the centre of the façade. This is adorned with ornamental features including the typical pediment supporting the characteristic Nabataean pinnacle. That *hypogeum* was surely used as a *triclinium* for funeral banquets.

It seems that in Byzantine time, the *hypogeum* was turned into a Christian church, judging by some inscriptions on the rear wall and the presence of some crosses.

The **Corinthian Tomb**, not very far from the Urn Tomb, even if very badly damaged, shows evident analogies with Al Khazneh's structure. The lower section consists of seven parts divided by eight semicolumns. Each of the hypogea, which are separate and of varying sizes, has a different style of doorway. The reason for this architectural choice is still unknown. In any case, the decoration of the façade again combines elements of both Nabataean and Roman design: the six lower central columns bearing a gable, above which are resting two gables acting as corner stones, and a central *thòlos* (a circular domed roof supported by columns).

It can be argued that this tomb, devoted to king *Malkus* II, has many features in common with the Triclinium of the Obelisk Tomb.

Another splendid tomb, not only for its architectural style, which in

---

*The Corinthian Tomb - **details of the typically Nabataean urn.***

reality is now hardly recognizable, but for its incredible colouring on the rock carved façade is the **Silk Tomb**. It is also known as the Rainbow Tomb due to the effect and variation of the different coloured horizontal rock bands of the façade.

For this reason it is presumably the most striking tomb among those similarly characterized by rectangular shaped pediments with a double cornice and protruding lintel, and double columns ornamentally placed on the outer edges.

Another important example of the craftsmanship of rock carved buildings is the **Palace Tomb**. This building is presumably an audacious imitation of a Roman palace, such as the palace of the Roman emperor Nero, the famous Golden House. However, if that were the case, it would make it one of the most recent constructions of the entire city, although this has not yet been finally established.

It is composed of three levels, but while the lower one was cut from the

rock, the others above were partially erected with blocks of rock, in order to compensate the insufficient height of the original rock face in relation to the impressive architectural plan.

The façade is curiously structured in such a way that the levels above are not as high as those below, creating an illusion where the higher storeys appear further away than they actually are. Consequently, when viewing the entire structure from below, an evident sensation of gran-

*The **Corinthian Tomb** seen from the Colonnaded Street.*

The Silk Tomb.

*The Silk Tomb: **the characteristic coloured bands of rock.***

deur and stateliness prevails.

Further on, almost attached to the external city-walls, is the **Tomb of Sextus Florentinus**, dating 130 A.D., and erected because the Roman Proconsul, after which it was named, had expressed a desire to rest forever in this land after his death.

There is much information regarding this funeral monument and its occupant. In actual fact, above the entrance a faded but still legible inscription declares in Latin: "To Sextus Florentinus, to the son Lucius, to the Triumvir for the minting of the coin, to the Military Tribune of the first Legion of Minervium, to the Quaestor of the Province Achaia, to the Tribune of the Plebs, to the Commander-in-chief of the Eighth Legion Hispania, to the Propraetor of the province Arabia, to the dearest father, Papiria erected this tomb according to his testament".

Its general condition has very much deteriorated, but we can still notice the usual elegant combination of Nabataean and classical features which are visible on the façade that, unfortunately, faces North and is rarely lit by the sun, appearing lacklustre in comparison to the other tombs.

Not far beyond is the **Carmine Tomb**, so called because of the purplish red shades of the rock which intertwine with other blue and white bands on the façade in a preciously decorative manner.

The inside of the tomb also presents the same splendid chromatic nuances of the rock.

The Palace Tomb **is one of the most monumental rock carved buildings in Petra.**

Al **Deir** provides a wonderful mountain top view of the city's central zone. The modern name for this site and of the building that is located here means Monastery. This can be explained by the fact that during the Byzantine period this Nabataean monument was used as a place of veneration by the Christians. The route up towards the Monastery is strenuous, but well worth the challenge and in any case there will be several chances to rest viewing the beautiful landscape and admiring the various tombs also present in this area.

One such example is the **Lion Tomb**, that takes its name from the two lion low reliefs that flank its entry gate, but which are now unfortunately severely eroded.

Its façade is typically Nabataean. The entrance to the hypogeum is adorned with semipillars that support a lintel decorated with a Doric frieze in designs consisting of Medusa heads, carvings and geometrical patterns of concentric circles. Above, there is again a gable, adorned with the usual Nabataean style pinnacle. The unusual "keyhole" effect was caused by erosion resulting from to the passage of wind between the entrance gate and the small window above. The interior of the hypogeum reflects the typical outlay of the triclinia. Immediately to the left, placed in a niche, there is

Arrival at Al Deir Monastery.

a block of rock dedicated to Dushara.

The steep path continues. A small detour will lead to **Qattar ad-Deir**, a large rock ledge, near which is Petra's only ever full water tank. It is often so full that moisture seeps out among the ferns and moss bushes into a sandstone grotto.

Approaching the summit where the Monastery stands the panorama is increasingly breathtaking. It will be possible to see the **Hermitage** caves, two cavities in the rock on the peak of a sheer pinnacle, decorated on the inside with a series of Christian crosses.

Proceeding still further the rock path reaches its narrowest point before finally opening into a vast platform with, protruding on the right hand side, the imposing façade of the **Al - Deir** monumental structure inserted between two gigantic cliff walls. After Al - Khazneh, this is the best preserved monument in Petra. Some scholars describe it as the tomb of *Rabbel* II, and as the most recent great Nabataean testimony. In reality this memorial is a great temple which was designed with the space opposite purposely flattened to act as a vast artificial platform to contain the large crowds of pilgrims visiting the holy site.

If one considers the dimensions of this building, its width being of about 50 meters, its height reaching 45 meters and the entrance alone being about 8 meters high, there is no doubt that a structure of this size had great importance for the Nabataeans as a place of veneration and pilgrimage.

The façade is on two levels and adopts the same architectural and decorative form as the Khazneh. The lower level is adorned with characteristically hook shaped Nabataean

*The Lion Triclinium, **so called for the two lion low reliefs that flank the gate.***

Al Deir Monastery **is one of the best preserved monuments in the city. Its colossal dimensions make it the biggest architectural complex of the area.**

capitals on semicolumns and by two lateral niches. The upper level consists of a broken pediment with a central *thòlos*. They are all decorated with alternating vertical bars and small circles in relief.

One can observe how the height of the building has been architecturally accentuated by the continuity of the central lower columns with those of the upper level, delimiting the broken pediment and leaving space for the *thòlos*. The style slightly excels the architectural tradition which associates the elements of Roman and classical architecture with Nabataean taste. Also, the way in which the central lintels are so strangely rounded, almost seems to herald the characteristic architectural features of Baroque style.

The single big internal chamber receives light from the entrance and on one side is the traditional niche that originally housed the rock statue of the god to whom the temple had been dedicated.

Al Deir Monastery -
the urn in detail.

"Building by carving: a population of sculptors"

The relatively soft rock of the mountains that form Petra's territory was an important basis for the development of Nabataean rock carving art: their motto was "building by carving" and from that starting point this people developed one of the most innovative building techniques, working directly on the raw material, which was easily at hand, and without moving it from its place of origin.

In order to do this the building had to be planned in a precise section of the mountain and adapted to the natural features. It had to be globally developed and it could not be modified to accept improvements once the work was in progress. This implied having a plan that had to be studied in all its minimal details. The proportions had to be calculated with extreme precision and each stage of the work had to be foreseen without mistakes, or there was the risk of obtaining a different final result to that which had been designed.

In this manner the work would develop in its definite and decorated format making it impossible to add elements once the task had finished.

The Nabataeans were, therefore, skilful designers and engineers, even if this seems rather unlikely for a people of nomadic tradition.

Nevertheless, they must have had at their disposal excellent craftsmen, perfectly capable of utilizing adequate and surprisingly sophisticated equipment for that period. This workmanship can be appreciated by just observing the perfect smoothness of the numerous Al - Deir columns. Similarly one can study the Unfinished Tomb to comprehend the several building phases and the planning foresight of this people.

A l-Habis massif (the Dungeon) lies directly behind Qsar al - Bint building. The route up is a gentle ascent in comparison to that which approaches the Attouf Ridge, and leads to the ruins of the ancient **Crusader Fort**, presently consisting of the remains of the walls, some passages and rooms, dating back to the beginning of the 12th century. The majority think that it was abandoned by the Crusaders after a sorely felt defeat suffered in the bloody Hittin battle in 1187. Along the way we will see the **Unfinished Tomb**, which, as the name suggests, interestingly reveals the engineering methods employed by the Nabataeans: they would first chisel a vertical wall in the mountain side, then, from its top, they would cut a ledge just wide enough for the skilled workers to engrave the highest parts of the façade. The craftsmen, then, descended to where a window or a door was planned, at which point the stonecutters would dig a tunnel as deep as the room required.

Then, they would either carve their way up to the planned height of the ceiling, or would cut away blocks of rock from the area that would become the floor.

Another interesting rock building in this area is the so-called **Colombarium**, an ancient Nabataean tomb, which has several hundred small niches presumably employed to hold the urns containing the ashes of the dead.

However, this is not the only suggestion, because it is argued that those cells were designed as nesting-boxes for pigeons, hence the name given to this unusual structure. In this case it would be dated after the Nabataean period, precisely in the Byzantine era. However, this latter hypothesis is not very convincing, considering the scale of the commitment in relation to its function.

Below – *The Colombarium,* **an unusual construction, the exact purpose of which is still unknown at the present time.**

Right – *The Colombarium - a niche in detail.*

Djebel Umm Al-Biyara

The **Umm al -Biyara** massif stands out behind Al - Habis and overlooks all the city. Its walls are so sheer making it appear impossible to reach the top, but approaching it from the South-West side one can get to the peak by a rather steep pathway. On the Eastern side of the mountain there are numerous tombs that offer a very wide range of Nabataean architectural styles, covering a period of 300 to 400 years.

At the summit, which is about 1158 m. high, the visitor will be impressed by the sight of many cisterns. Their presence gave the mountain the name of "Mother of Cisterns", which is what Umm al Biyara means. The cisterns, carved in the rock, have a curious bell shape and an access hole that was covered by stones, effectively hiding their presence from strangers.

It was here that the remains of a very ancient Edomite settlement were discovered. Many scholars think that this site must be the mythical village of **Sela** ("Rock") referred to in the Bible, from which Petra would have then taken its name. It was thought to have existed for about 50 years during the 5th century B.C. before being annexed by the Nabataeans who then lived there for some time. This would be supported by the presence of a small temple on this plateau.

The ruins of the village are located in the far Eastern side from which a broad flight of steps leads to the very edge of a sheer drop where one can admire, being very careful, the city below. Close by, a statue representing a god was discovered. This could have been the site of a temple, an ideal place from where to hurl offerings or sacrificial victims: this, too, can be considered like a "High Place of Sacrifice".

In the area North of Petra, precisely in the Turkmaniyeh valley, there are other interesting tombs. Among these there is the **Turkmaniyeh Tomb**, where we can notice that the lower part of the façade doorway has been removed by the effect of violent flooding of the water course that flows nearby. However, the typical Nabataean structure of this tomb is still visible; it also consists of a characteristically Assyrian turreted top which is decorated, in the lower part, by a double cornice separated by capitals and supported by double square shaped columns placed at the sides.

The main reason why this tomb is very famous is the long inscription in Nabataean language inscribed on the upper part. It certifies the sacredness of that site devoted to the god Dushrat, in such a terminology not dissimilar to legal jargon. This is the translation by Wiegand: "This tomb and the large and small chambers inside, and the graves made as loculi, and the courtyard in front of the tomb, and the porticoes and dwelling-places within it, and the gardens and the triclinium, the water cisterns, the terraces and the walls, and the remainder of the whole property which is in these places is the consecrated and inviolable property of the god Dush-Hara". The text was then completed by Brunnow:"......nor shall any man be buried in the tomb except him who has a written contract to be buried according to the said writings relating to the consecrated things, for ever".

At the back of this tomb a small valley leads to the Roman built **Conway Tower** from which the Northern part of Petra was controlled.

The ruins of this bastion, with the Arab name of Al - Mudawwara ("the rounded"), are still visible at the northernmost point of the city wall

Some of the narrow passages carved out of the rock. They gave access to the tombs situated in the highest parts.

that protected Petra, near the *Wadi Nasara*. Its English name derives from Agnes Conway, an archaeologist who was working on the ruins of that area in 1929 together with the man that would later become her husband, Mr. Horsfield.

Near the *Wadi Nasara*, it is possible to admire the complex of tombs known as **Mughar al-Nasara Tombs**. These were the tombs of the Christians that lived in Petra, authenticated by the name *Nasara* which is the Arabic translation for *Nazareth*. Therefore, it is presumed to have been a type of ghetto for Christians; this hypothesis is reinforced by the several crosses carved on the walls and entrances to the tombs.

Almost all the funeral monuments display in the upper section the unmistakable turreted top of Assyrian origin, and on one of them we can see the capitals that ornate the gap between the upper and lower cornices. This particular solution serves as evidence of the so called intermediate phase of stylistic evolution of local rock carving expression, which tends to join classical stylistic features with the still solid architectural Nabataean traditions. However, the atmospheric elements have so severely damaged the accurate carving of most geometrical and floral patterns, designed to ornate some lintels, that nowadays almost everything has disappeared.

Close by is the **House of Dorotheus**, which consists of a group of openings in the shape of windows or doors, on which Dorotheus' name is inscribed twice in Greek. It was probably the dwelling of a wealthy citizen and his large family. The Triclinium is interesting for its dimensions (12 m x 10.50 m), which make it one of the biggest of the entire Middle East.

A Swiss man in Petra: J. L. Burckhardt

In 1812, a young Swiss explorer, Johann Ludwig Burckhardt, an enthusiastic student of the Arab civilization and member of the "Association for promoting the discovery of the inner regions of Africa", set off for Africa in order to explore the source of the River Niger.

He accurately prepared himself for the journey, for example adapting himself to a survival level vegetarian diet, and accustoming his body to deprivation. He knew Arabic and had already perfected his conceptions on Islam after a stay in Syria and Jordan.

During the journey from Damascus to Cairo, approaching Palestine and Egypt he heard of legends told by the natives regarding the incredible ruins of a dead city protected by the mountains surrounding the Wadi Musa.

In his desire to verify the reliability of those tales he devised a plan which would enable him to investigate the area without arousing any suspicion. In actual fact, the local Bedouins that had often never seen a European, were renowned for being very suspicious and hostile towards strangers. However, Burckhardt thought that, like all human beings, these people when faced with the opportunity of a possible earning would not have minded being approached.

He wrote in his diary: "....I, therefore, expressed my wish to sacrifice a goat in honour of Aaron at his tomb, which I knew was located at the end of the valley; in this way I thought that heading for the tomb would enable me to visit the valley." So, he disguised himself as an Arab and, having taken the name of Ibrahim ibn Abdallah, he hired a local guide to take him to Aaron's tomb.

Everything went according to plan: the Siq and the spectacle that appeared before his eyes were absolutely unique. However, if he had wandered too freely among the ruins, he would have made his guide suspicious. Therefore, he only examined Al-Khazneh and the Urn Tomb which were sufficient evidence for him to realize that this was the city he had heard of, and he wrote in his diary: "....the Wadi Musa ruins very probably belong to the ancient city of Petra." Notwithstanding the excitement of what he had just discovered, Burckhardt stayed in that area only one day. His was the first testimony of the existence of that legendary city given to the Western world. It was 22nd August, 1812.

Jabal Harun

This area of mount Al - Barra is considered sacred to the Muslims, and tradition has it that here lie the remains of **Prophet Aaron's Tomb** (Jabal Harun).

The shrine was entrusted to Greek-Christian monks until the 13th century. Then, when it became a Muslim holy place, it was restored by Sultan Qalawun. The present domed complex was built in 1459.

Every year a goat is offered as sacrifice during the commemoration of the failed sacrifice of Isaac by his father Abraham (Eid - al - Adha).

This place is pervaded by a solemn aura of spirituality.

There exist localities imbued by the vital spirit of the saint or hero that had lived there. The spiritual presence and power are continuously renewed by the chant of prayers from each pilgrims in this holy site.

If ever a location generated a vigorous, indefinable and ageless sense of the power emanating from the venerated virtues of a saint, this is surely the place where Aaron is buried.

Sabrah

Sabrah is rather distant from the centre of the city and, judging by the remains of what appears to be the barracks, it must once have been a garrison that was possibly used by the Roman soldiers employed to defend the Southern entrance of the city. Alternatively, the barracks could have been used as accommodation for mine-workers, since there are several copper mines in that area. We can also find a series of temples, a bridge, the ruins of a wall and a fortification located on a plateau above.

The most interesting remains for visitors are some columns coated with plaster and painted deep red. There is also a small Roman theatre carved from the mountain side near the embankment of the *Wadi El Sabrah* river. The theatre is semicircle shaped with eleven concentric levels and was able to hold about 500/800 spectators.

This theatre was probably used for *naumachia*, which were naval games such as those held in ancient Rome in the present day Navona Square. The water would have arrived from specially created channels constructed to divert the Wadi El - Sabrah flood-waters, caused by periodic rains which would have otherwise destroyed the crops in Petra.

They collected part of that water in a reservoir and cleverly directed the overflow by pipe into the theatre arena. The theatre was made water-proof by using a type of putty, the remains of which are still visible, and was filled with water to host naval games until the heat of the sun finally evaporated the reservoir. During the rest of the year the theatre reverted to staging normal performances.

Heading back towards the city, do not forget to look out for the **Snake Monument** (El Hayye). It is located on the summit of a protruding piece of rock, above a *djin*, a block of squared rock. It is coiled up on itself and its head points South-West. It should not be forgotten that for the Nabataeans the snake symbolized continuity, therefore, eternity.

The archaeological site of Al-Beidha

North of the Forum Hotel, outside Petra the ruins of the ancient village of **Al - Beidha** can be visited. This, together with Jericho, represents the earliest archaeological site of the Middle East. It dates back some 9000 years and was excavated by courtesy of the archaeologist Diana Kirkbride who was in charge of a series of excavations from 1958 to 1983. The work was intended to prove that this location was one of the few that preserved evidence of the transition period of the human species. This consisted in the passage from a nomadic style, when man subsisted on hunting, to a settled phase, when he survived on domesticating animals and cultivating the land.

The settlement is constructed on several levels, seven precisely, counting the Mesolithic one which has now been reached. Each of these levels features various differing style houses, artisan workshops and copperwork furnaces. These are the remains of the earliest Neolithic buildings found to date. Their shape was circular and their structure was supported by central posts, similar to the technique used for wigwams. They had thatched roofs covered with a thin layer of clay.

An interesting finding which was dug out during the excavations is a clay seal, probably belonging to an Edomite king, bearing an inscription of Phoenician origin, which is in some parts incomprehensible. It should date back to the 7th century B.C. and is without doubt the first Edomite inscription ever found.

A rather big room is still visible: it has a central part surrounded by other buildings along its perimeter and it could have been a type of "factory", as the remains of stone and bone tools, axes, grinders and polishers have also been found. Other interesting discoveries are the big grinding querns, the re-

mains of stone walls and paved floors.

On the way back to Petra, the ruins of another Crusaders' Fortress can be noticed: that of **Al - Wu'eira**. There are still some of the external walls of this fort that during its troubled history was occupied several times.

The Muslims conquered the fortress in 1144 by massacring the Frankish garrison which was stationed there.

The very young king of Jerusalem, Baldwin III, burnt all the trees in the nearby valleys in an attempt to recapture the position and induce the Muslims to surrender. This manoeuvre was very unpopular with the Muslims because, according to the rules of Holy War (or *jihad*), the destruction of trees is forbidden.

Later the fortress was again in the Crusaders' hands and was further strengthened. A group of Italian archaeologists, from the Universities of Florence and Urbino, studied the complex of fortifications erected by the Crusaders in the area of Petra. They came to the conclusion that this fortress was part of a defensive network to which the Crusader Fortress of Al - Habis also belonged. Like the latter it was abandoned rather early, following the defeat suffered by the Crusaders in the Hittin battle which was fought in 1187 and which marked the relentless advance and predominance of Arabs in that territory.

Al Beida **is, together with Jericho, one of the most ancient archaeological sites of the entire Middle East.**

Tomb at the entrance to the Siq that leads to Al-Barid.

A brief excursion outside the city takes us to what we could call a Petra in miniature: **Al - Barid**. This is now also a small ghost-town, which was once the main caravanserai located North of Petra. It acted as a depot for goods which were traded in the city and lay directly on the main route that led to Arabia.

Access to Al - Barid is similarly gained through a mini Siq: at its entrance is an enormous water tank, one of the several Nabataean ones which is still used by the Bedouins, and a temple also used as a tomb. This site is not very popular with tourists. For this reason one can experience a feeling of solitude and spirituality when walking along the various paths that lead to its tombs and, who knows, also capture the mystery and presence of those people that once lived there.

The whole area is strewn with funeral buildings, houses and monuments. Among the best rock designs is without doubt the **Painted House**, mainly for its interior. It is a *triclinium* finished with plaster walls, decorated with flowers and grapevines, with Cupids chasing each other among the branches.

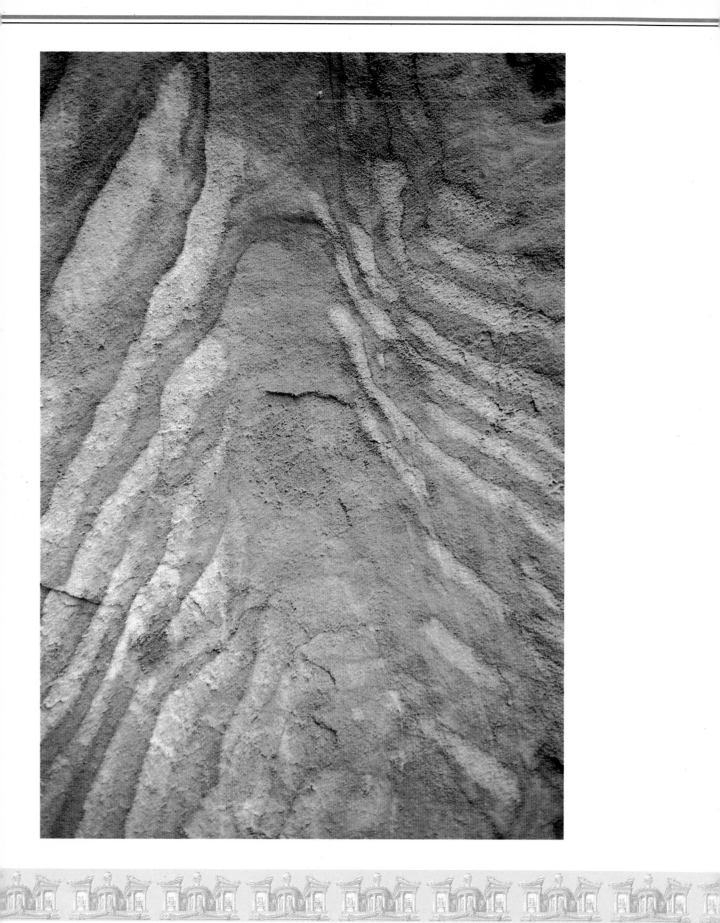

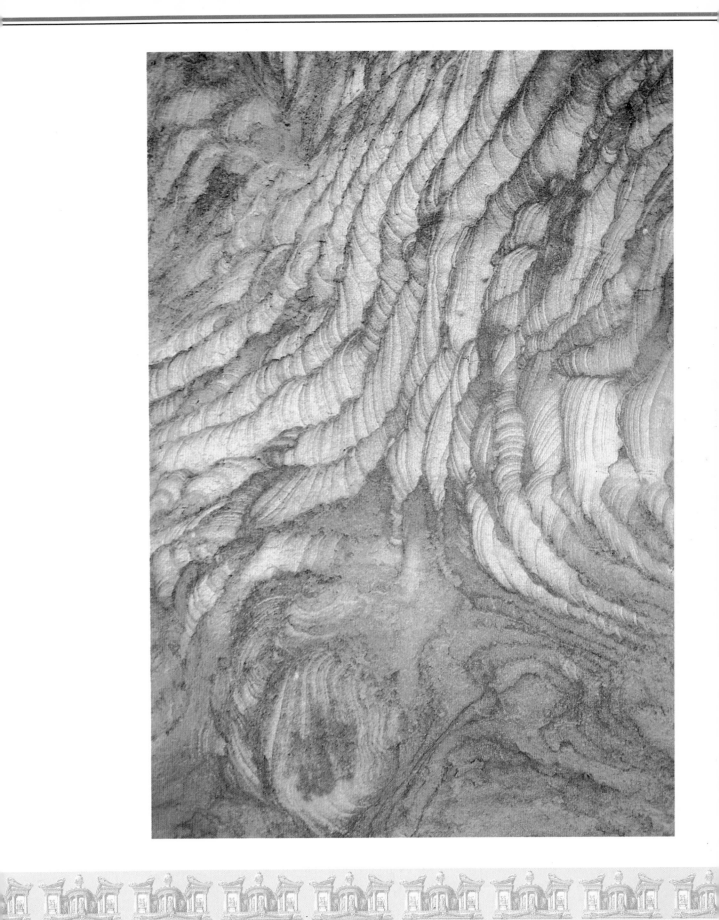

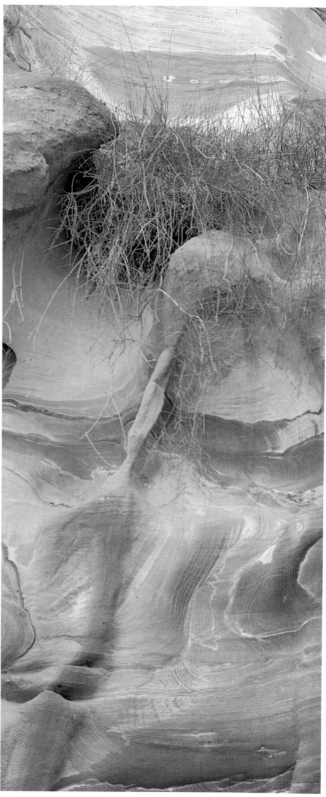